ROMAN CAMBRIDGESHIRE

DAVID M. BROWNE

GW00566815

THE OLEANDER PRESS OF CAMBRIDGE

The Oleander Press
17 Stansgate Avenue
Cambridge CB2 2QZ

© 1977 David M. Browne and The Oleander Press

ISBN 0 900891 09 2

i

Cover illustration:
Flagon from the Water Newton Silver Hoard

Title page illustration:
Bronze Horseman, Willingham Fen Hoard

Designed by Ron Jones

Printed and bound by Burlington Press, Foxton.

ROMAN CAMBRIDGESHIRE

Introduction

Since Cyril Fox wrote his masterly *Archaeology of the Cambridge Region* (1923) considerable advances have been made in our understanding of the Roman occupation of the former counties of Cambridgeshire and Huntingdonshire. The most startling has been the revelation through aerial photography of the extensive colonisation of the fenlands with its many square miles of native farmsteads and accompanying drainage schemes. Less spectacular but equally important is the discovery by the same technique of the intensive occupation of the river valleys of the south and west. New villa estates as well as native farms have been revealed and it is now possible to appreciate the settlement context into which previously isolated finds of pottery and other artifacts must be fitted. Intensive excavations in the Nene valley have traced the development of that important industrial region. Work at Godmanchester and Cambridge has established the history of these small towns. Research at the latter sites and at Longthorpe have allowed a reconstruction of how the region figured in the early years of the Roman conquest.

However despite all this excellent endeavour there is much to be learnt as only a fraction of the sites have yet been sampled. Although a few books and articles deal with specific areas and topics no comprehensive account has been attempted.

Roman Cambridgeshire aims to summarise the present state of our knowledge of the region's political, economic and social development. It is concerned to show how archaeological research has contributed to the picture. Wherever possible I have tried to bring the evidence together in a chronological account. The present state of knowledge does not always allow this when dealing with economic and religious matters and here I have been content to use selected examples to indicate the scope of activities in the hope that future investigations will place them in their full historical context.

Historical Background

There are no direct references in the ancient authorities to events in the county

LONGTHORPE

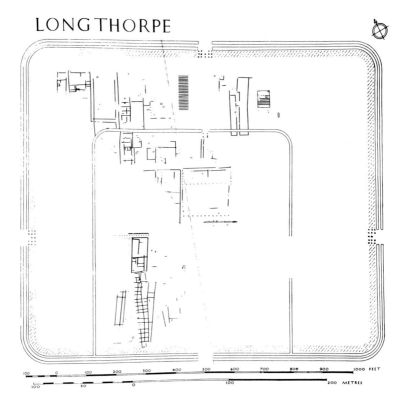

1. Plan of the fortress at Longthorpe *(Courtesy of Professors S.S. Frere and J.K.S. St. Joseph)*

during the early years of the Romanisation of Britain. However combining archaeological evidence with interpretations of certain passages in authors such as Tacitus allows us to reconstruct an outline of military activity in the region.

The advance of the Roman army to the Trent and Humber was spearheaded by Legio IX Hispana and several auxiliary units. These may have traversed the west of the county by several routes: a principal one seems to have been the valley of the Great Ouse. A convenient ford of the river occurred north of Godmanchester, and to the south of this on a gravel island about 30 feet O.D. an early fort was established. Excavation has shown that the south side of this fort was defended by two ditches and a timber and turf revetted rampart. The south gate lay on the site of the later *mansio* (lodging-place on the imperial highway) and along this side there was at least one four-post interval turret. The long axis of the fort was orientated east to west. Inside were

4

found traces of a probable granary and other timber buildings. A native settlement that sprang up outside the defences is evidenced by an oval hut. The fort was earlier than the first road surface of Ermine Street but the road from Sandy, indicating the line of advance, seems to have been contemporary, running beyond the fort further north-east along the Ouse valley. This was 10 metres wide between its side ditches. It is to be expected that garrisons were established in the lower Nene valley at the same time and possibly also at Cambridge.

In 48 A.D. the governor Ostorius Scapula in preparation for his advance into Wales issued an order to disarm all natives within the province and in allied territories. This was resisted by the Iceni of East Anglia and others and Scapula with a force of auxiliaries fought a successful engagement against them at an earthwork in the area, sometimes identified as Stonea Camp. The base at Longthorpe near Peterborough may have formed a key element in his arrangements after this incident to control the intercourse between the Iceni and their northern neighbours particularly the Coritani of the Midlands. It was also strategically sited as a rearward reinforcement to the Fosse Way frontier. The fortress was located overlooking the river Nene on its south-west. Although it must have been serviced by roads, particularly one leading eastwards into the fenland, the local road system as it now appears seems to post-date its abandonment.

The earlier fortress was enclosed by two ditches and an internal rampart and measured 360.5 metres east-west by 301.95, an area of 10.9 hectares (27.3 acres). It was south-facing and the internal buildings were, contrary to normal arrangements, orientated across its width. This orientation was maintained in the reduced fortress which was enclosed by a single ditch and rampart measuring 201.3 metres east-west by 219.6, an area of 4.4 hectares (11.0 acres). The north and east gates of the first phase of the fort at Longthorpe were excavated and consisted of two carriageways separated by two posts and flanked by six-post guard towers that projected forward of the actual gate setting. In the reduced installation the northern *porta decumana* (the main entrance of the camp farthest from the enemy) was a simple passageway with a first-storey tower over the gatebridge. The *retentura* (the area behind the principal buildings) of the first fort contained a series of structures including auxiliary barracks, a courtyard building which may have served as a stables or parking area for baggage animals, a granary, a smaller store building for other foodstuffs, and possibly traces of two *praetoria*, or quarters, of the auxiliary commanders. The principal structure was the *principia* (headquarters) with a courtyard and basilica and beside the latter was the *praetorium* (commander's house). In the *praetentura* (the area in front of the principal buildings) two legionary barrack blocks were traced. The evidence points to the garrison of Longthorpe I being composed of the first cohort of Legio IX

5

and two other cohorts along with two units of auxiliaries, one infantry the other cavalry. It seems that Legio IX Hispana was split at this time into three separate detachments *(vexillationes)*. Finds of armour and other equipment including the iron cheek-piece of a helmet attest the legionary presence. A fragment of an iron parade helmet probably belonged to an auxiliary cavalryman.

An important ancillary feature of the Longthorpe fortress was a works depot sited 500 metres east of its south-east corner. It was established on the site of an Iron Age farm which was cleared away by the army before it began work on the depot. Pottery kilns were the main feature. Most of these were surface built, probably with turf walls, although there were also standard updraught kilns. The ware produced was red with a pinkish surface. The forms were of Rhenish origin, the potters having come across with the army, and included flagons, small jars, *mortaria* (bowls for grinding foodstuffs), pots made to imitate the imported samian ware and cheese presses.

The rather irregular arrangements of the fortress suggest that it was hurriedly constructed during a campaigning season. The historical context for the reduction of the fortress seems to be the Boudiccan revolt 60-1 A.D. Petillius Cerealis, legate of Legio IX, rushed to encounter the rebels and in a disastrous engagement had his infantry cut to pieces, escaping only with his cavalry. It seems from reinforcements sent to the legion after the rebellion that only part of it was involved, presumably that closest to the theatre of war. Thus Cerealis may have been operating from Longthorpe. After his defeat, left with a severely reduced garrison, he was forced to make emergency arrangements for its defence and to do this he reduced the perimeter of the fortress excluding most of the *retentura*. No time was available for new building and the earlier installations were maintained. As soon as the rebellion was put down the fortress was abandoned and Legio IX regrouped at Lincoln.

At some time before the Boudiccan revolt the fort at Godmanchester had been abandoned and on its site a civilian settlement grew up along the newly-constructed Ermine Street. This was destroyed by fire, probably by the rebels. Natives who had co-operated with the Romans bore the brunt of their fury.

The post-Boudiccan military arrangements of the region are unclear. A garrison must have been left in the Nene valley and it is perhaps to this phase that the auxiliary fort at Water Newton belongs. This has not been excavated but covers two hectares (five acres) with a double-ditch system and a third at the south-west corner. It controls the Nene crossing and was the establishment that was called *Durobrivae* "the (gated) enclosure at the ford or bridge". Another military site with ditches, pits and cremations which contain pots made in the Longthorpe works depot has been identified at Lynch Farm. Its context is unclear but it may be contemporary with the fortress. South of the county at Great Chesterford (Essex) a large fort/fortress

2. Aerial view of the fort at Water Newton *(J.K.S. St. Joseph, Cambridge University Collection, copyright reserved)*

may represent post-Boudiccan arrangements. The Flavian situation (69-96 A.D.) is also uncertain although it seems that the supposed fort at Cambridge was then established and we may presume that some military presence was maintained in the Nene.

The economic and settlement history of the region is dealt with below. Direct evidence of political and military matters is very slight for the following centuries. A small police force of troops may have been scattered through the settlements of the imperial lands of the fens if a sword from Whittlesey, a bolt of a ballista (or spring-gun) from Cottenham and the Witcham parade-helmet can be taken as evidence of such.

The second century was one of peace and development in which a money economy became widely established. Sporadic coin hoards may represent nothing more than local incidents or votive deposits. The end of the century was more unsettled and some private estates may have been confiscated by Severus because of their owners' support for his rival Clodius Albinus. With the Severan rearrangement of the province the county may have been split between the two new provinces *Inferior* and *Superior* with the Fen Causeway as the boundary.

In the third century a period of economic retrenchment set in, in many areas accentuated by difficulties in controlling drainage and the general uncertainty in the Empire, particularly acute from the formation of the Gallic Empire in 259. Barbarian raiding became an increasing threat and coin hoards of the period 270 to 282 are common. In the later third century Godmanchester was walled and at the end of the century there is evidence that the town was sacked and part of the population massacred.

The reigns of Diocletian and Constantine saw considerable reconstruction undertaken. Roads were restored, such as that between Cambridge and Godmanchester, attested by two milestones from Girton. There was relative prosperity for much of the fourth century punctuated by reverses caused by temporary economic and military problems. Such a passing difficulty may have caused the walling of Cambridge in mid-century and occasioned the deposition of a gold coin hoard at Durobrivae (Water Newton), circa 350. Thirty coins in a leather purse were put in a bronze bowl and this fitted into a pot. Two folded silver vessels were placed on top of the purse inside the other containers. The whole was covered with a pottery lid. Considering the value of the hoard the owner must have been a wealthy inhabitant of the town with much to lose.

The area must have been affected by the barbarian depredations of 367. The addition of bastions to the walls of Godmanchester and Durobrivae are attributed to the restoration policies of Theodosius. Roman civil life maintained itself in the province into the first decades of the fifth century. Its increasing uncertainties are reflected by the notable increase of hoarding in the late fourth and early fifth centuries. In this phase Continental soldier-settlers seem to have been imported into the area to guarantee the security of the population in line with policy elsewhere in the Empire. Pottery and metalwork attests their presence at Durobrivae and Godmanchester. By the third decade of the fifth century most of the Roman economic system had collapsed. The Nene valley pottery industry was dead. Sites were abandoned in considerable numbers although, as at Cambridge, there is no evidence that this was the result of conflagration or massacre. Much of the population may have continued to subsist in the area to become assimilated in part with the increasing number of Continental settlers as the century progressed. If the accounts of St. Guthlac's weird encounters in the fens are any guide it would seem that a distinct British population survived into the seventh century.

Waterways

The landscape of Roman Cambridgeshire differed from that of the present in several important respects. Most of the claylands bore oak forest. Roman agriculture was beginning to make serious inroads into this by the end of the occupation. The drainage pattern of the fenland was entirely different.

3. The Car Dyke at Goose Hall, Landbeach, looking northwest

By a remarkable series of cuts and canals Roman engineers assured the agricultural development of this zone. Except for the Lynn Ouse all of the eastern fen rivers should run naturally into the Well Stream and hence enter the sea via the Wisbech outfall. However a series of artificial cuts have directed the waters to the Lynn outfall. Most of these cuts are probably Roman, particularly that from Littleport to Brandon Creek and the artificial Little Ouse from Decoy Fen to Brandon Creek.

The ancient and modern courses of the river Cam coincide in the main between Cambridge and the Newmarket Railway bridge, Ely. From Ely to Littleport the present course is a recent cut. Previously the Cam was a tidal river up to Ely and down to the Middle Ages navigable as far as Cambridge.

The natural drainage to the south and east of the Cam between Wicken and Wilbraham consisted of a major stream with a dendritic pattern of tributaries from the fen edge. This stream flowed northwards, parallel to the Cam and then made a west turn to join the latter near Upware. The Romans dug a series of lodes that interrupted this stream and diverted the waters to the Cam before their natural confluence. Bottisham Lode, Swaffham Bulbeck and Reach Lodes are definitely Roman and Wicken Lode, Monk's Lode and Burwell Old Lode are probably of the same date. The lodes served for transport and drainage. That to Reach may well have been concerned with the exploitation of clunch quarries. The importance of the waterways in bulk transport should be borne in mind, especially building materials from the limestone areas north of Peterborough such as Barnack.

The river Snail originally ran north to reach the Lark and has an artificially altered course which is probably Roman. The pattern of cuts and natural streams connected to the Lark east of Prickwillow include Roman ones.

The major engineering work of the south of the county is the Old Tillage often called the Car Dyke. From Waterbeach to Setchel Fen, Cottenham, runs a dyke with a flat bottom flanked with banks. It is now thought to date to the earlier second century and to have been used into the second half of the fourth. The Old West River between Lockspit Hall and the Cambridge road bridge, Ely, was not in existence in the early Roman period and the Old Tillage formed the link between the Cam and the Ouse. It seems that the Old West came into existence as a result of overflowing during third-century flooding. The Old Tillage is the southern end of a chain of waterways ultimately linked to the Lincolnshire Car Dyke. The suggested routeway is from the Old Tillage to the Ouse and on via the Colne Ditch, Cranbrook Drain, West Water (old course of the Ouse), the extinct waterway south of Whittlesey island connected with the West Water, the King's Dyke, Oakley Dyke and Fulham Dyke and finally via the Nene to the Car Dyke. Twenty four lamps probably from the watercourse south of Whittlesey may represent part of a cargo being carried on a barge along this system.

The Lincolnshire Car Dyke is also a flat-bottomed canal flanked by two banks, although there is only one bank, on the east, as it approaches the Nene. North of Peterborough it is over 17 metres wide by one and a half deep. The west section of Cnut's Dyke was probably operating in or before the third century and continued in use until possibly the early Saxon period. Water transport was of considerable importance to the potters of the Nene valley for distributing their wares to the army and their local market in the fens.

The Rodham Farm canal has a close association with part of the course of the Fen Causeway as the latter runs on its north levee. The canal is the earlier feature and it was succeeded as a transport link by the road in the later Roman period probably after the flooding and silting of the third century had made it difficult to use. The Flaggrass waterway is an artificial drain that is linked to the Rodham Farm canal.

Roads

The courses of the roads can be seen on the map. The earliest was probably that from Sandy to Godmanchester where it was established during or soon after the garrisoning of the fort. Ermine Street post-dates the abandonment of the fort at Godmanchester but was in use before the Boudiccan revolt. It was probably constructed soon after the establishment of the part-legionary base at Longthorpe. It was resurfaced in several sectors many times during the Roman occupation. The stone piers of a bridge to take it across the Nene have been found. King Street leaves Ermine Street north of the Nene crossing and rejoins it at Ancaster. It was built probably soon after Ermine Street as a more direct route. The Fen Causeway may not have formed a continuous road until the later Roman period. Its relationship with the Rodham Farm canal suggests that at least a late surface was subsequent to silt deposition by the canal in the third century. The road may have taken over the transportation function of the canal once the latter had become defunct as an active waterway. However at its western end it may have been built much earlier as part of the army's attempt to control contacts between the Iceni and Coritani. At Aldwincle (Northants.) a timber bridge showing three separate phases of construction and rebuilding had horizontally-piled timber abutments revetted with piles and carried a road to Leicester across the Nene. The 'Via Devana' at Godmanchester seems to post-date the early Flavian land divisions. It was probably formally established with the fort at Cambridge. The other roads radiating from Cambridge are undated but may have been built at the same time although the road to Horseheath may belong to the second century and there are indications that Akeman Street north of Cambridge did not form a continuous system until the later Roman period. The short spur road from Great Chesterford to the Icknield Way at Worsted Lodge was probably built to give access to Icenian territory for the garrison in the large fort established after the Boudiccan rebellion. An alternative road between Sandy and Godmanchester, replacing much of the earlier one, was constructed at the end of the Roman period.

Settlement History

Most of the county in pre-Roman times was part of the lands of the Catuvellauni. The Nene probably formed the boundary with the Coritani to the north and it is likely that there was an ill-defined border with the Iceni in the east fens.

In southern Cambridgeshire the very early Roman settlement pattern was similar to that of the pre-Roman Iron Age, occupation being confined primarily to the river valleys and the edges of the chalklands. The aftermath of the Boudiccan revolt may have led to some depopulation in the district. In the latter part of the first century the local population may have been increased by an influx of settlers from the Low Countries.

The second century saw a rapid expansion of settlement which reached a peak in its second half. The expansion was particularly marked in the fenlands and is thought to have been the direct consequence of government action under Trajan and Hadrian. The official element is noticeable particularly in the large-scale drainage works undertaken. There had been some colonisation by Catuvellaunian entrepreneurs from the Verulamium area (modern St. Albans) in the later first century in order to exploit the salt resources of the Wash district. The forms of settlement show that native Britons comprised the bulk of the colonists in the second century. As the population and economy expanded so the previously military site of Cambridge took on the aspect of a market and administrative centre for the southern area. There was additional colonisation in the north fens during the late second century which is supposed to have come from a Low Countries source.

During much of the third century there was a contraction of the area of settlement though not necessarily a decline in population which may have been more concentrated: the main reason was a widespread freshwater flooding at the fen edge. There is good evidence at the southern skirtlands of the movement of settlement to higher ground during the period 230 to 270 A.D. when flooding spread from Willingham West Fen to Stretham. There were also waterlogging problems in the north fens, the Nene and the Ouse valleys which the drainage systems were inadequate to cope with. Difficulties in the Empire at large were probably responsible for the lack of co-ordinated effort needed to deal with these natural problems. There was a parallel decline in the number of occupied settlements to the south of the fens.

The area undoubtedly benefited from the Constantinian reconstruction programme in common with the rest of the province. This was a period of relative prosperity as can be seen in such things as utensils and house fittings. In the north fens there was a tendency towards the consolidation of settlements into larger units. Waterlogging again became a serious problem in the south fenland during the later fourth century causing a limited abandonment of settlement.

Occupation is attested throughout the area well into the fifth century although there is little continuity with Saxon settlement. The breakdown of the drainage systems with the consequent decline in the utility of agricultural land must have led to a gradual depopulation of the fenland. Elsewhere the picture is similar, with settlements of recognisably Roman types fading out in the fifth century. In the mid-fourth century Cambridge had been walled but this defence does not seem to have been maintained and excavations have shown that during the next century the site became deserted and overgrown with vegetation.

Towns

Cambridge (Durolipons)
In the late first century B.C., Catuvellaunian settlers created a village on the

Castle Hill spur. This settlement has been traced through three structural periods in the most important of which the huts were contained in oval enclosures. The last village was abandoned at the time of the Roman conquest. It is not clear what function was served by the various features of the early Roman period, but they may have been connected with a military garrison. The most important was a palisaded enclosure. These were superseded in the last quarter of the first century by an enclosure to the west of, and aligned on, the Godmanchester road. The enclosure may have been a fort: it consisted of a ditch, renewed at least once, with a simple entrance gap and a cobbled forecourt by the road. There was a cobbled area in the interior but no structures were traced. Any buildings may have been of timber founded on horizontal members.

In the first half of the second century the whole area of the fort was redeveloped. All previous installations were obliterated and a set of cambered gravel streets with the Godmanchester road as their axis were laid out, creating *insulae,* regular blocks of land defined by streets. Several houses and yards were built. The houses were rectangular and built of timber and daub. Some had tiled roofs and floors with hearths were made of chalk, gravel or cement. One house had a clay-walled oven in its yard. The area also contained rubbish and latrine pits. Some houses were replaced within the second century by new buildings. The part of the later walled area to the east of the Godmanchester road does not seem to have been much developed at this time.

In the third century many houses were abandoned. Their sites were used for refuse disposal in pits and large caches of pottery denoting some organised form of dumping have been found. Marl quarries were dug and there was intensive gravel extraction on the west side of the hill. However a few new houses were built and occupation also continued in some of the earlier ones.

The houses continued to be occupied during the fourth century up to the time of the construction of the defences. In the earlier fourth century, gravel extraction was intensified in the western area. In the mid-fourth century over 8 hectares (19.8 acres) of the settlement were enclosed by a wall and ditch. This does not seem to have been well maintained and may have been only a response to a temporary emergency. The ditch was 10.7 metres wide at the top with a flat bottom 3.35 metres wide at a depth of 2.44 metres. The wall was built of limestone, clunch, flint and bonding tiles and was 2.74 metres broad, backed by a rampart over 9.14 metres wide at its base. Behind was a gravel *intervallum* road: a street immediately behind the defence-rampart. The west gate had projecting towers and, apparently, guardchambers. At the same time the streets within the new walls were remetalled and new houses were built, some of which possessed polychrome wall plastering.

The eastern area was developed for the first time in the fourth century with the construction of huts, yards and pits. Across the river in the area of

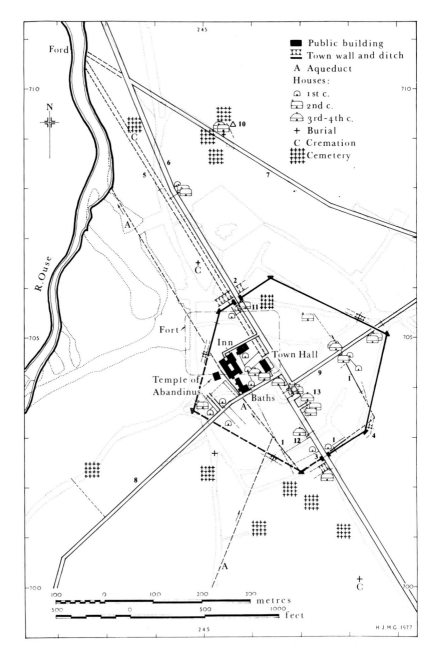

4. Plan of Godmanchester c. 290 A.D. *(Courtesy of Mr H.J.M. Green)*

St. Sepulchre's was a small settlement possibly connected to the Roman bridge by a wooden causeway. This may have acted partly as a small industrial quarter as pottery wasters of late third or early fourth century date have been recovered there.

The site continued to be occupied until the end of the century. It was gradually abandoned during the fifth century and vegetation and soil grew over the derelict areas. It became what Bede was later to describe as a *civitatula desolata*. There is no evidence that the town met a disastrous end.

Godmanchester (? Durovigutum)

The settlement destroyed by the Boudiccan insurgents was replaced in the early Flavian period by one laid out according to a regular system. The land was divided by ditches into strips 96.1 metres wide, probably a local variation from 300 Roman feet. There were two orientations, one either side of Ermine Street though neither at right angles to it. The strips were regularly sub-divided according to a traditional Celtic measure of land division. Adjacent to the town on the gravel terrace was an area of 108 hectares (267 acres) of infield cultivation comprising fields and droves linked to the highways. Over this zone is evidence of town rubbish being used for manuring. The more remote gravel areas and adjoining boulder claylands were used for rather dispersed outfield cultivation covering an area of at least 288 hectares (711 acres). Pollen evidence suggests that a greater area was under arable cultivation than was used for meadow.

In the area adjacent to Ermine Street the settlement comprised a series of crofts containing agricultural structures such as two-post drying racks, long hearths and circular ovens for corn-drying, rectangular threshing-floors and pottery storage-jars held in wicker and timber bins. Crop remains indicate the consumption of spelt, bread or club wheat, emmer and six-row barley. The settlement pattern was essentially linear along Ermine Street, which was refurbished at this period. The Cambridge road seems to post-date the land division. Two types of building are found: one the round hut built of wicker and daub or turf and the other the rectangular house of timber with spaced uprights filled with wattle and daub, a thatched roof and earth floors.

Just after 120 A.D. the existing structures on the west of the town were demolished and work begun on a *mansio* complex. This and the centre of the town were contained within a trapezoid enclosure of 8.06 hectares (19.9 acres) delineated by a V-shaped ditch 3 metres by 2 metres deep with its sides revetted by wattle. Ermine Street was reconstructed to a width of 12 metres and a wooden bridge may have been provided for it over the north side of the ditch. To the north of the town it was re-sited, presumably to a new bridge over the Ouse. Minor roads were constructed within the town. Soon after the work on the *mansio* was under way it was suspended for a

5. Reconstruction of the Baths at Godmanchester *(Courtesy of Mr H.J.M. Green)*

while and when it was restarted the plan of the bathhouse had been changed to two baths rather than one, perhaps to segregate men from women. The total length of the *mansio* was 95 metres. The inn building in its final plan had an entrance on the north into a yard flanked by stableblocks. The visitor then proceeded through a corridor into the inner courtyard which had a range of guest rooms on its east and west sides and to the south a large room, an audience-chamber, diningroom and kitchen with a tower granary. The inn was constructed with masonry footings and ground storey. The upper storeys were half-timbered. Several rooms had polychrome plastering and tessellated floors, while there were mosaics in the south range.

To the north east of the *mansio* was an aisled barn and outbuilding that may have housed the slaves. South of the inn was the bathhouse. This was connected to Ermine Street by a road suggesting that it also acted as a public baths. A dyke supplied it with water and also functioned as a drain. The area of the *mansio* was fenced off in the early third century.

A·shrine to a local god Abandinus stood to the west of the *mansio*. The dedication occurs on one of several bronze votive feathers found in a late third-century rubbish deposit. It is inscribed and says, in translation: "To the god Abandinus Vatiaucus gave this from his own resources". The earliest temple was a timber-framed rectangle 5 metres by 7, built in the second century. This was later replaced by a timber-framed rectangular structure surrounded by a wooden portico. As the shrine was included in the third-century fence around the *mansio* the two were probably intimately connected. The rubbish pits of the *mansio* produced two pipeclay Venus statuettes and some had dog burials which may have been sacrifices. A *temenos* (sacred enclosure) gate and wall of another temple have been identified in the south of the town.

In the town of the second century two new types of building appear, one the mud or cob two-roomed cottage, the other a timber-framed structure, open-fronted and often acting as a workshop. A late first-century to early second-century workshop in the north of the town contained shaft furnaces for iron smelting and in its first phase also produced bronze objects. The linear pattern of settlement was retained, with cremation cemeteries along the roads beyond the occupied area. The population towards the middle of the century is suggested as about 200. At this time the site suffered a temporary setback caused by a widespread fire.

The town was provided with more pretentious civic buildings in the early third century. A hall of single-aisled basilican plan (24 metres north — south by 12.9) was built in Barnack rag and flint at the centre of the town. A second aisle was inserted later. It encroached partly on Ermine Street which was realigned and resurfaced. An open area in the centre of the town defined by two roads may have acted as the market place. There seems to have been a reduction in the density of settlement in this century. The lower-lying areas around the town suffered from the widespread contemporary phenomenon of waterlogging.

In the later third century the town walls were built enclosing an area of 10.91 hectares (26.95 acres) within an irregular hexagon. The wall was backed by a clay rampart and fronted by a U-shaped ditch, 4.9 metres wide and 1.8 metres deep. The north and south gates, probably constructed after the walls had been erected, had rectangular gatetowers with solid lower storeys flanking an arched central carriageway and two footways. There was a simple postern in the west wall.

At the end of the third century the *mansio* and bathhouse were destroyed by fire. To the south-east were found disarticulated human bones which had been gnawed by dogs. It would seem that the town was sacked and its population slaughtered. In a pit outside the south front of the bath building, probably dug during clearing-up operations on the site, was found a hoard of objects from a woman's jewel box. These comprised a gold chain and pendant with crude human masks *en repoussé* in a filigree setting, an intaglio gem depicting Ganymede and the eagle, two intaglios with a blue surface showing

Mercury (?) and a draped woman, and a cameo of devitrified glass with a silver coating. Associated with these were four plain bronze finger rings, a silver ring, a bronze pin, two bone pins, a fragment of a shale bracelet and sixty coins, forty of them barbarous radiates. The latest coin was an *antoninianus* (debased silver coin) of Allectus, 293-6. A date of c.300 seems likely for the deposition.

Fourth-century buildings are not frequent in the town. Elsewhere, as witnessed by milestones from near Girton, reconstruction was taking place in the early fourth century. Any revival at Godmanchester seems to have been limited. A third temple to Abandinus was built over the old one in mid-century, polygonal in plan with a timber façade and masonry footings. In its centre was a stone tank, later replaced by a well. To the east of the temple remains of bone-working for caskets were found in the enclosure ditch of the *mansio*.

In the late fourth century the *mansio* and basilica were robbed presumably for the refurbishing of the defences in the Theodosian reconstruction. A bastion for artillery was added at the south-east corner of the wall and a new ditch dug 11 metres wide. The west tower granary of the inn and the north part of the bathhouse were still in use in the last years of the century, and the bath continued to function into the fifth. The site of the *mansio* was enclosed and two timber structures erected within. Early Saxon pottery may have belonged to the occupants. By the end of the century the old roads were in a state of disrepair but a new road to Sandy may have come into use at this time. Pottery finds have suggested that a complement of Germanic soldier-settlers may have been present in the town at the end of its life as a Roman centre. There was a fenced enclosure in the east of the town from which has come an Anglo-Saxon pot among late Roman material.

During the life of the town private estates grew up beyond its outfield. The owners of these may well have been dignitaries of the town. At Rectory Farm there was a courtyard enclosure 50 metres square of mid-second-century date with a timber-framed building on its east side. In the third century a stone structure with mosaics and painted plaster was constructed near the south-east corner and in the early fourth century a corridor villa was built on the same alignment to the north. At Huntingdon two stone structures were erected in the early third century on a site occupied during the previous century and these were later connected to form one winged villa more than 40 metres long.

Water Newton (Durobrivae)

The town of Durobrivae was formed from the *vicus* (civilian village) that had developed alongside the auxiliary fort there. When the army moved away many of the traders and retired soldiers and their families had become so well-established as to feel no need to follow the troops.

The defences constructed in the second century or later formed an irregular six-sided enclosure taking in a large part of the ribbon development along Ermine Street that had been created in the first two centuries. The defences consisted of a clay bank with an associated stone wall. Bastions were probably added in the late fourth century. There was a flood defence bank on the north-east.

The interior was not subdivided into regular *insulae*. Instead lanes led off Ermine Street to demarcate irregular areas full of stone and timber buildings usually of the shop-house type with their gables end-on to the street. A courtyard building near the centre of the site may have been a *mansio*. Another substantial building is implied by an inscription which may contain the names of local officials.

The name of the town is given in the Antonine Itinerary and is confirmed by the mortarium stamp CVNOARDA FECIT/VICO DUROBRIVIS. A milestone of Florian (276 A.D.) records the mileages from the town. The mortarium stamp shows that Durobrivae was regarded as a *vicus* and may be compared with Petuaria, Brough-on-Humber. It is thought that the town may have achieved the status of a cantonal capital.

The site shows signs of intensive occupation and rebuilding and has an associated industrial and commercial quarter of over 100 hectares (250 acres) which included the former location of the fort and Normangate Field. These had begun in the Flavian period and attained their maximum development in the fourth century by which time Durobrivae was the flourishing centre of a prosperous region.

Inscriptions from Sawtry and Thrapston may mark the limits of the official territory of the town and the Welland may have been another boundary. To the east and south-east are a series of ditched enclosures which probably formed part of the infield cultivation of the settlement.

Villas

Several villa complexes are known in the river valleys and along the fen edge in the south of the county. Very few have been excavated.

Occupation near Arbury Road, Cambridge, was spread over seven acres and spanned the years 130 to 400 A.D. The principal structure belonged to the fourth century and was an L-shaped masonry building the main part of which had a tile roof with a later annex covered with ragstone tiles. The building was heated and plastered inside and out. The annex was internally decorated with a pattern of red and white panels. There were other masonry buildings on the site probably replacing an earlier set of timber structures. At various dates the area was occupied by working floors, wells, pottery kilns, storage and rubbish pits and a cemetery of cremations and inhumations which included a stone mausoleum incorporating stone coffin burials.

Nearby to the north at King's Hedges was another major complex which had pre-Roman origins and a complicated sequence of structures and land divisions. One rectangular masonry building may have started as a religious structure. It was aisled in plan with a tessellated floor and may have been associated with carved limestone architectural pieces found in later pits and wells and a stele of a war god. It dates to the second and third centuries and its use was ended by a fire. The derelict building was converted in the fourth century into a domestic structure with living-rooms and a kitchen disposed around a courtyard with tessellated floor. In the later fourth century the building along with others stood within a large rectangular double-ditched enclosure.

A number of villas are found along the southern chalkland border of the fens at Isleham, Landwade, Fordham, Burwell Castle and Reach. At Landwade, Flavian timber huts were replaced by a timber aisled barn house in the early second century. This was rebuilt in stone in the late second century and a bath suite inserted. There was a complete reconstruction in stone in the first part of the third century when the bathhouse was modified and a dining-room with a mosaic built. The building was destroyed by fire in the early fourth century. At Reach the plan was of the so-called winged-corridor type. The wings had a projecting apse on their façade and the south-west one incorporated a bath suite. A heated dining room was located at the centre of the rear range. The building was of flint with brick quoins. It included rooms with tessellated tile floors and polychrome wall plaster.

The villa at Grantchester incorporated stone columns, while of those at Comberton and Litlington, one had a bath suite and heated rooms, and the other had a courtyard-type plan with more than thirty rooms including a bath range and mosaics and was associated with a walled cemetery. At Ickleton there were a corridor-type house, a basilican building and another structure. At Guilden Morden there was a rectangular house with a bath-suite within a court with an associated stone barn and gatehouse.

In the far west at Great Staughton in a tributary valley of the Ouse there was a winged corridor-type villa with geometric mosaics and painted wall plaster. 865 coins ranging from A.D. 306 to 362 were found, many of them minims and minimissimi, which were very small coins based on the radiate crown series of the Gallic Empire. There was a second winged house to the southwest of this, converted in the fourth century from the north-east corner of a second and third century courtyard structure, the rest of which was demolished. The corridor and some rooms contained mosaics and heating was provided by channelled hypocausts in two rooms and a pillared hypocaust in another.

20

The villas of the Nene Valley are best described in their most developed phase around the middle of the fourth century. By this time they can be found spaced along the valley at an average separation of about 1½ miles. The bigger villas were often at the heads of valleys tributary to the Nene, with smaller structures up-valley in positions indicating that they might have belonged to the tenants of the larger estates. The villas are mainly sited on rising land of clay or cornbrash and their territories would have included access to running water, water meadow and woodland.

The most advanced structures architecturally are found in close proximity to Durobrivae. These are the two structures at Water Newton, two villas at Ailsworth, the courtyard villa of Mill Hill and the *praetorium* at Castor. However this is no necessary criterion of economic status, as the very prosperous farm at Hall Farm, Orton Longueville, testifies.

Lynch Farm, Orton Longueville, is an example of a major farm complex with half-timbered structures, an aisled barn, stockyards and fishpond. In common with other farmlands of the district, which were plagued with difficulties with the watertable, the lands of this farm were drained by ditches. The site also contained a late Roman family cemetery and what may have been a Romano-Celtic temple. The indications are that cattle raising was especially important exploiting clay and alluvial pastures.

Stone-flued corn-drying ovens were very widespread in the third and fourth centuries, for example at Hall Farm and Lynch Farm.

Fenland Settlement

It is likely that much of the fenland was imperial property. A stone from Sawtry inscribed PVBLIC . . may mark its boundary on the west. The large-scale drainage works indicate official action. However there is no sign of overall planning and layouts seem to have been dictated in the main by the topography. Several types of settlement have been recognised in the area. In the late first century there were a number of small irregular layouts fitted into an environment of freely moving streams. These employed small short drains and were often scenes of industrial activity. Loose agglomerations of small farms occur in some areas. Large irregular settlements were formed by an accretion of small farms into extensive agglomerations in the second century. More regular layouts were a feature of the second half of the second century, while from the middle of the century combinations of earlier irregular and new regular arrangements are found. Compact groupings were another major category. Some combine irregular and regular elements and those which last to the end of the Roman period were quite extensive. As time went on there was an increasing tendency for population to concentrate in several fairly large centres. There is no doubt that it is legitimate to see the fenland landscape as being occupied by some individual farms but more often by small hamlets of two or three sites, larger ones of four or six, and by villages of seven or more. Villas are virtually absent in the fenland proper. One is found at Tiled House Farm, Stretham. However around the borderlands of the fens, at such places as Hockwold in Norfolk, villas are found in close association with villages suggesting some sort of manorial arrangement. A few sites seem to have acted as more than just agricultural communities. At Flaggrass a variety of finds and what may have been a store of querns suggests that the site acted as a trading centre. Bullock's Haste, Cottenham may have been an entrepôt on the Old Tillage and was an important local centre of the imperial cult, to judge from the find of a bust of Commodus (176-192 A.D.).

The majority of the farmers in the fens would have been smallholders leasing their land from the imperial government for short terms. The area would have been under the control of a *procurator saltus* (procurator of public lands) and the rents would have been farmed by *conductores*, or contractors.

The skirtlands which contained several villa estates were probably privately owned although some properties in the north-east of the county may have fallen into imperial hands as a result of confiscations under Septimius Severus.

In the Nene valley the number of small peasant farms is comparatively small in relation to areas like the Welland valley. The presence of the army and the growth of villa estates were probably the causes. It has been suggested that the expansion of Romanised settlement in the valley forced out smallholders and that it was they who formed a significant proportion of the population involved in the expansion of settlement on the fen siltlands during the second century.

Most of the settlements of the Great Ouse valley have a pre-Roman origin. They are noticeably sited to be in close proximity to the river, the main transport link, just above inundation level. Occupation is particularly concentrated at the mouths of the small tributaries that debouch into the Ouse, as for example at Holywell and Somersham. The types of settlement show a strong continuity with those of the fens. The houses were rectangular with wattle and daub walls set on wooden sleeper plates. Most had beaten earth or clay floors although roughly tessellated ones are also found. Earthenware and stone tiles as well as humbler vegetable materials were used for roofing. A few properties even had glazed windows.

A form of building that recurs in the county in agricultural units is the aisled barn which is found both as an outbuilding in a villa and as a principal farm structure. Commonly animals and residents were billeted under the same roof. In the Nene valley they are rectangular with their length usually twice the breadth and a similar proportion of nave width to aisle. The footings are of stone while the upper walls are of cob and timber. Posts

6. Aerial view of the settlement at Bullock's Haste, Cottenham *(J.K.S. St. Joseph, Cambridge University Collection, copyright reserved)*

were used for the aisle divisions. The door was normally in the long side. In the south an aisled building is associated with the villa at Ickleton. At Landwade Roman-style fittings were incorporated at one end in the second rebuilding expressing traditional residence habits in a new cultural form. An aisled barn built in the second century formed part of the *mansio* complex at Godmanchester.

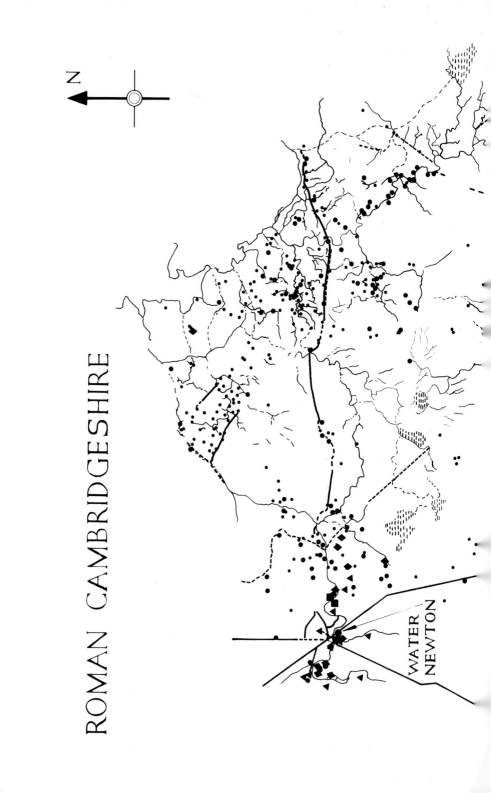

ROMAN CAMBRIDGESHIRE

N

WATER
NEWTON

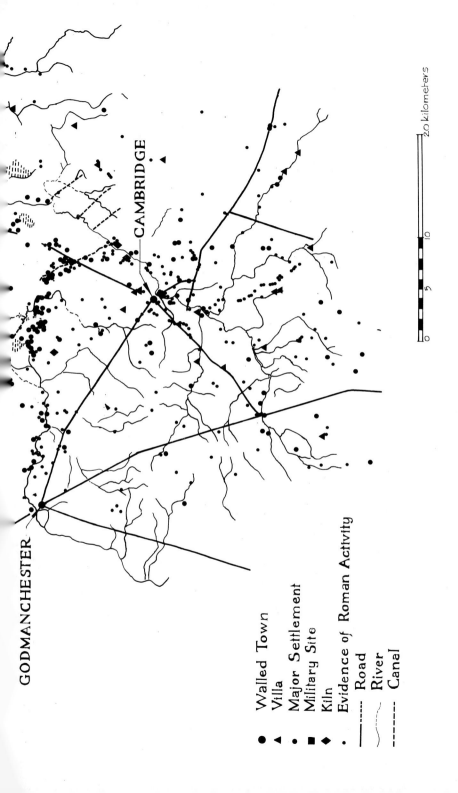

GODMANCHESTER

CAMBRIDGE

● Walled Town
◀ Villa
• Major Settlement
■ Military Site
◆ Kiln
· Evidence of Roman Activity

······ Road
〜 River
------- Canal

20 kilometers

0   5   10

Agriculture

Two main types of field system are found in the area. The most prevalent is of pre-Roman origin, the so-called Celtic fields which are small, irregularly disposed, and associated with a mixed cattle and arable economy. In the fens they are often found with a characteristic settlement nucleus consisting of a double enclosure approached by a drove. The house stood in the inner enclosure while the area between the two was used for holding wintering stock overnight. The other type was regular and rectilinear, reflecting Roman practice and associated with cereal production. In some parts the regular layout supersedes an earlier irregular one suggesting a reorientation of the local economy but this is the exception not the rule. The standard fenland holding has been estimated at 110 acres of ditched land (nearly the Roman standard unit of 200 *iugera*=125 acres).

The fenland economy, like that of many of the river valley settlements such as those of the Great Ouse, was a mixed cattle and arable economy with the emphasis decidedly towards cattle-rearing, as both good wet and dry pasture were readily available. Cereals were raised for home consumption. Cattle products, particularly leather, were supplied to the army in the north of Britain, a trade in which the canal system figured prominently. The dampness of the land made sheep-rearing less viable although sheep predominate in the earliest phase of siltland settlement, declining sharply in relation to cattle in the second century. The finding of pottery cheese presses on many sites emphasises the importance of dairy products in the subsistence economy. Both sheep and cattle were valued for their milk in Roman farming. Loomweights attest the production of cloth, perhaps supplied to the army. Horses were raised for the army and for eating.

Spelt and hulled barley were the most commonly-raised cereals. In the later Roman period, in response to deteriorating weather conditions, corn-drying kilns appear on many sites. Other sources of food included fish, eels, oysters and wildfowl. Reeds and peat were cut for fuel and building.

A scythe from Abington Pigotts and a plough coulter from Wimblington are examples of the types of agricultural implement in use. Quernstones for grinding cereals occur on many sites. The principal stones, probably imported ready-made, were lava from the Rhineland, Hertfordshire puddingstone, Millstone grit and various sandstones.

Salt extraction was a principal motive for occupation of the silt fens in the first century A.D. This activity had ceased by the mid-second century. Sites near March, Elm, Manea, Wimblington and Whittlesey have yielded pits and trenches for evaporating brine, and debris in the form of baked clay trays or cylinders, supports and linings.

The Uses of Stone

It is valuable to examine the building materials used in the Godmanchester baths and elsewhere to appreciate how local stone sources were exploited in the Roman period and how the county participated in a province-wide trade in finished and unfinished articles. However it should be appreciated that, for the majority of construction purposes, timber was the main material. Wood was also used for many household vessels and implements, boats and coffins. A wooden hairpin was found at Horseheath.

The flint used at Godmanchester would have been gathered from the surrounding fields and was available elsewhere from the Upper Chalk and boulder clay. Chert obtained at Cottenham was used for buildings at Willingham. Generally available gravel and sand was dug for floors, yards and cement.

A sandstone used at Godmanchester closely resembles the ferruginous

7. Sculpture of Lion from funerary monument at Girton in Ketton stone *(Courtesy of the Museum of Archaeology and Ethnology, Cambridge University)*

27

pebbly grit found in the Lower Greensand at Silsoe (Beds.) although this is not the only possible source as outcrops occur along the Lower Greensand into Norfolk where it is termed carstone.

The Corallian outcrop at Upware provided a limestone for building which was used at St. Ives, Somersham, Houghton, and as far as the Great Staughton villa. The Cam-Old Tillage system must have provided the means of transport.

In the Nene valley stone quarries were opened up from the second century. Here the main stone used was the local cornbrash. At Barnack the ragstone, a shelly limestone, was extracted. This was used in building at Godmanchester and was exported as far as London. Another major use was for coffins especially in the fourth century when the finished article was sent to places like Cambridge. Also in the Nene, limestones were exploited at Wittering and Sibson and a marble at Alwalton. A local guild of sculptors was operating in the lower Nene valley. It was responsible for the lion and stag group from a funerary monument at Durobrivae and the two charioteers of the funerary monument at Bedford Purlieus. Statues of Minerva and Hercules were carved at Sibson.

Quarries at Ketton (Rutland) provided an oolitic limestone which was used at Godmanchester baths and in the villas at Comberton and Ickleton. It was also the material for the Girton funerary monument depicting a lion devouring a deer or calf.

Roof slates were obtained by surface quarrying of limestone at Colly-weston (Northants.). They were used in the Nene valley from the first century and earthenware tiles do not become common there until the third century. Collyweston slates were widely used both in the county as at Godmanchester and beyond at Irchester (Northants.) and Great Casterton (Rutland).

Several important sculptures and architectural blocks have been identified as being of Northants. limestone without further definition and among these are a male torso from Girton, the "war god" sculpture from Arbury, a frieze or cornice at Arbury, and a column base from Grantchester.

Chalk was employed as a building stone in several of the southern villas. It was also used for tesserae and spindle whorls. Quarry pits have been found at Burwell and Cherry Hinton. Chalk and limestone provided the raw materials for mortar and plaster. In the south limekilns have been identified at Fulbourn, and in the Nene at Helpston.

Most villas and several lesser establishments including town houses possess plastered walls with polychrome designs. Several schemes are found but common features are plain panels and panels and zones of imitation marbling above a dado (the plain lower border of a wall painting). These are in the full Roman tradition although it is likely that local craftsmen did the work. More ambitious designs, which attest the desire of the client to identify himself closely with Roman fashions, are known from villas such as Ickleton where

8. Sculpture of ? a War God from Arbury, Cambridge *(Courtesy of the Museum of Archaeology and Ethnology, Cambridge University)*

9. Sculpture from Arbury Road, Cambridge (*Courtesy of the Museum of Archaeology and Ethnology, Cambridge University*)

the walls were decorated with foliate patterns and representations of the gable end of a building and the foot of a life-size figure. The peasantry of the county may have remained intensely conservative but the landowning class shows every sign of having been assimilated to the general Roman culture of the province.

Several kinds of stone were imported from some distance to provide finer architectural fittings. At the Godmanchester baths wall-linings of Purbeck marble and Hopwood "marble" were used. The former, from the Isle of Purbeck, was a highly polished shelly limestone. The industry was active between 50 and 150 A.D. The latter, a Carboniferous limestone, was extracted near the river Derwent in Derbyshire, possibly as a sideline to the exploitation of the Derby lead resources. A red oolitic limestone from Leckhampton Hill, Gloucestershire, was used as a door sill.

The West Country seems to have been the home of the mosaicists employed at the baths judging from the materials they used for tesserae. The grey limestone came from the Purbeck area while the cream ones were from the Inferior Oolite of Frocester Hill, Gloucester, and the Lias of Stowy Quarry, Somerset.

A local guild of mosaicists based at Durobrivae was operating in the Nene valley in the third quarter of the fourth century. Their products, geometric in design, are found in Lincolnshire but only at the *praetorium* and the Mill Hill villa, Castor, in the Nene valley.

Personal ornaments of stone were imported from other parts of the province and the Continent. From York beads, armlets and pins of jet were obtained. The Isle of Purbeck industry supplied shale bracelets. The amber beads in the religious hoard from the Hempsalls, Willingham, are of uncertain origin. A brilliant orange sardonyx intaglio showing a sporting Eros came from Shepreth. This is a Hellenistic piece and may have been a family heirloom brought by a settler into the country. Cornelian and clear quartz beads are known from Litlington and Haslingfield respectively.

Pottery

The centres of pottery production in the south of the county and parts of the fens showed a strongly conservative spirit. Pre-Roman forms survived well into the second century and vessels in native-style fabrics can be found throughout the period. Several small-scale factories were operating at places like War Ditches, Cherry Hinton, Milton and Over during the Flavian-Trajanic period. War Ditches produced two major classes: one was an oxidised ware decorated by rilling and scouring and some burnishing. The forms were large, narrow-mouthed, medium-mouthed and wide-mouthed jars and imitation Gallo-Belgic platters. The other class consisted of the more delicate beakers, usually with a cornice rim in a buff or cream fabric and decorated *en barbotine* (applied as one might ice a cake) with panels of dots or circles and dots. The latter class imitates Continental forms and may be the work of immigrants. The eastern area was supplied at this time from Norfolk kilns while other parts received early Nene valley products. The mortaria used in grinding foodstuffs were imported from kilns near Verulamium at Brockley Hill and Radlett.

The Hadrianic period in south Cambridgeshire saw the emergence of the Horningsea kilns and others in that vicinity. These attained their maximum output in the second half of the second century. The products were marketed on a scale intermediate to the localised distribution of the earlier small centres and the county-wide distribution of the mass producers of the Nene valley from the later second century onwards. It was the expansion of settlement in the second century that gave Horningsea the market it required. The kilns varied in form with features such as circular or oval plans, movable domes of clay plates, internal piers supporting fire-bars and some had properly arched flues. The ware was usually a sandy grey-brown and the most characteristic form was a large storage jar with double rim and decoration by combing and point punctuation. Other shapes included jars, bowls, platters, indented beakers, lids, lamps, a few pedestalled jars and mortaria.

While Horningsea supplied the south fens and other southern parts, the east fens continued to receive products from Norfolk and the west fens from the Nene valley and some local producers. A small pottery industry was maintained in the Ouse valley. Four or more kilns operated at Fen Drove, Earith, producing pottery, mainly a coarse gritted jar, and tiles.

Norfolk also supplied the east fens with their mortaria while the other areas were serviced from Hartshill and Mancetter (Warwicks.) with lesser amounts coming from the East Midlands, Colchester and the Nene valley.

The main non-British import of pottery was samian, the glossy red ware made at several centres in Gaul. Most of the first-century supply derived from South Gaul, but from Hadrianic times Central Gaulish Lezoux ware predominated. In the later second century the area received an unusually high proportion of wares from East Gaulish factories and this emphasises the close contacts established from early days with the Rhineland. Other forms of Rhenish colour-coats had been entering the area since the first century. A fine incense burner from Litlington of second-century date comes from a Rhenish source and has the name INDU(L)CIUS spelt out in perforations on its body. Other foreign imports to the area include a lead-glazed vase in the Girton cemetery from the Rhone valley and a New Year lamp of first-century date from Guilden Morden cemetery.

The fens are notable in some features of their pottery intake. The population's limited aspiration to *Romanitas* may be reflected in the relatively

10. Nene Valley pottery beakers *(Photo by J. Scott, courtesy of Mrs J. Pullinger)*

11. Pottery from Cambridge *(Photo by J. Scott, courtesy of Mrs J. Pullinger)*

12. Samian vessels from Cambridge *(Photo by J. Scott, courtesy of Mrs J. Pullinger)*

small amount of decorated samian on the sites: amphorae are few and flagons rare. The finding of several late second-century amphorae at the skirtland site of Fen Drove, Earith, is unusual. Large storage jars are common and were needed to counteract the damp conditions, pits being unsuitable. Cheese presses recall the importance of dairying.

In the third century, Nene valley manufactures comprise some 90% of fenland pottery and although less dominant further south they are still in a significant majority. This trend is maintained in the fourth century. However some local factories maintained themselves, as for example that at Jesus Lane, Cambridge, where wasters of several vessel forms have been found. The fabric is grey and a most distinctive shape is a narrow-mouthed vase with a pedestal covered with a silver-grey slip. However, this factory may date to the second century.

A limited importation of red colour-coated wares made in Oxfordshire in the fourth century probably filled a demand for samian-style vessels and in the later part of the century characteristic *mortaria* from that region were obtained although three-quarters of the supply came from the Nene valley. Calcite-gritted wares from various sources were also used and so-called Romano-Saxon pottery is found in small quantities.

An intriguing sherd from Sawtry has a spearman painted in white on a black ground. Details such as his beard and brooch are in red.

Iron Age fabrics and forms also continued well into the Roman period in the Nene valley. The Roman army made use of local potters but also brought with it Continental colour-coated beakers and cups and South Gaulish samian. The Longthorpe unit had its own pottery field employing Rhineland craftsmen between 50 and the early 60's A.D. and some of these may have remained after the withdrawal of the troops to develop the local industry. Kilns such as those at Hardingstone, Ecton and Weston Favell on the Upper Nene provided most of the first century supply to the valley. Only a small amount was produced around Durobrivae, mainly jars and beakers in a light grey fabric with slashed cordon decoration. Around the turn of the century a kiln at Water Newton was making calcite-gritted jars.

The familiar colour-coat industry which made the so-called Castor ware started up in the second quarter of the second century. The main products were cups with stylised hunting scenes and beakers decorated *en barbotine*. These were sold to the army in the north as well as to civilian purchasers. The range of forms, including ones imitating samian, was broadened in the third century and many forms were manufactured with slight change until c.370A.D. It is thought that Rhenish potters may have been engaged in developing the colour-coat production.

In the early third century, kilns are known at Billing Brook and Stanground. At the latter, grey ware and black colour-coats imitating East Gaulish samian forms were made. The structure of a rebuilt kiln at Billing Brook illustrates one type found. The flue led into a round firing chamber. This had a tongue-pedestal projecting from its back wall with radiating clay bars stuck in it and attached to sockets in the kiln wall. A clay floor was built over these to support the pots with small holes in it to allow the hot gases to circulate in the kiln. Two other kilns were built of pre-fired clay blocks including their pedestals.

Around the middle of the century, works were operating at Stanground and Normangate Field where a network of small lanes facilitated the transport of clay, and in the late third century at Sibson and Stibbington. At Stibbington the late third-early fourth century kilns were associated with a workshop containing tanks full of clay. A flywheel was found in a well. Other pottery sites include Wansford, Werrington and Peterborough Cathedral. Among the non-colour-coated products of the industry were white ware mortaria with black grits, many grey wares and calcite-gritted pots.

The management of the marketing of the products was probably handled by *negotiatores,* whose guild headquarters is thought to have been the large establishment built at Castor c.250 A.D. Several detached buildings are disposed around a large court or garden; on the north is a substantial house, the "praetorium", containing mosaics, painted plaster and hypocausts; on the south is a bath block, while at the east end of the north wing was a *podium,* probably of a temple.

Tiles were produced locally and imported. Roller-stamped patterned box flue tiles from the large factory at Ashtead, Surrey, were used in the Godmanchester baths. The full range of Roman types was used in the buildings of the county including *tegulae* (flanged roof tiles), *imbrices* (semi-circular roof tiles), flue and *pilae* tiles (used to support the floor in underfloor heating) found in a variety of fabrics, the commonest being red, brown and calcite-gritted wares.

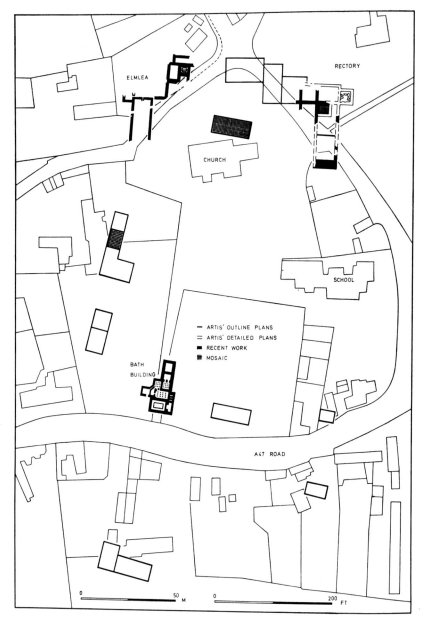

RECTORY

ELMLEA

CHURCH

SCHOOL

— ARTIS' OUTLINE PLANS
= ARTIS' DETAILED PLANS
■ RECENT WORK
▦ MOSAIC

BATH
BUILDING

A47 ROAD

0   50
                        M

0   200
                                FT

13. Plan of the Roman House in Castor village *(Courtesy of Dr J.P. Wild)*

Iron Working

Opencast mining of iron was undertaken in the Nene valley at Bedford Purlieus and Old Sulehay Forest. Near the former place a villa and workshop have been excavated. The industrial installations included a shaft furnace, and two bowl furnaces of mid-late second century date and the site was littered with slag heaps. The products were transported by a road connecting with Ermine Street. Sacrewell, Thornhaugh, was another important iron-working centre with a workshop and furnaces. Ovens of either a long-necked bottle plan or figure-of-eight plan which were probably smithing hearths are found at several sites such as Lady Lodge Farm, Orton Longueville, Lynch Farm and the Longthorpe late Roman farm. At Normangate Field there was an aisled workshop with over twenty furnaces and this factory was probably engaged in commercial production in contrast to the usual manufacture for home use. Elsewhere in the county there is sporadic evidence for local iron manufacture such as at Godmanchester, Flaggrass in the fens and Wendy in the south-west.

A wide variety of iron artifacts was employed by the population although not all were necessarily manufactured locally. Among these may be listed agricultural implements such as reaping hooks, plough-shares and coulters, the ubiquitous nail, knives, keys, shears, vessel chains, brooches in the early period, compasses and hipposandals (the last-named from Arrington and Wendy).

Ironworking hoards, such as that found just outside the county at Great Chesterford, have been interpreted as votive deposits during a pagan revival in the later fourth century.

Bronze Working

Bronze working is only occasionally attested in the region and many objects were probably imported. Bronze was more expensive than iron and was used for ornaments, higher-quality vessels and several other specialised implements.

A fine skillet comes from Prickwillow with a highly decorated handle showing mythical beasts, a genius, dolphins and a scroll pattern in niello. It is stamped BODVOGENUS F. and may have been used in religious rituals. Three bronze jugs from Hauxton of second- or third-century date may have come from a barrow burial. A vessel hoard of fourth-century date was found at Burwell and included bowls with *omphaloi* bases and a fluted bowl. The use of brooches by the common people belonged mainly to the first two centuries A.D. Later types such as the crossbow seem to have been worn by the well-to-do. Most of the normal kinds were in use including bow types, enamelled plate and penannular brooches. A fine example of a dragonesque brooch was found at Fengate. From Barrington there is a late gilt crossbow fibula. Bronze pins were used for clothes-fastening and for holding hairstyles in place. One with a garnet setting was found at Godmanchester and a late Roman spiral-headed type at Comberton. Needles, plaited and twisted bracelets, rings, styli, spoons, bells and casket fittings were also made in bronze. A late second-century signet ring found at Rectory Farm, Godmanchester, bore an intaglio in a dark blue paste with a representation of a young god or hero. An example of a locket was found at Godmanchester and an enamelled seal box at Arbury Road. A knife handle from Croxton is in the form of a hound chasing a hare. A mirror in white bronze was found at Orwell.

Other Metalwork

Silverware was the property of the wealthy. An engraved signet ring was found at Stilton and a finger ring with snake's-head terminals at Ditton.

Pewter was a lesser man's substitute for silver. The area is notable for the quantity of hoards buried. Most of it was manufactured in the West Country although some may have been made in East Anglia. Hoards like that from Isleham Fen comprise jugs, bowls, *tazze* (cups) and dishes. Fine jugs have been recovered at Roll's Lode, Quaveney and Burwell. The earliest find is a flanged bowl in a third century context at Arbury Road.

Lead was used for piping (Comberton villa) and coffin linings (Arbury Road). Lead tanks found at Huntingdon, Willingham, Burwell and Cambridge have been associated with Christian baptismal rites.

Glassware

Nearly all the glassware used was imported. Whole vessels are rare except in cemeteries where square or hexagonal green glass bottles were commonly used as cremation urns. There are several examples of imports from the large factories of the Seine-Rhine region, notably a pale-blue glass jug from Litlington of early second century date. From Egypt came the bowl in a Girton cremation in a clear glass with a slightly green tint whose base bears the incised representation of a duck and Nilotic plants. Other vessels used include unguent bottles sometimes buried with their female owners. Glazed windows were not uncommon in many houses. Beads and intaglio settings were also made from glass.

Boneworking

Bone was a commonly available, cheap substitute for several metal items. Local bone craftsmen were working at places like Cambridge, March, Godmanchester and Burwell. At Godmanchester bone inlay for caskets with ring and dot decoration was being made in the fourth century. Pins were made at Cambridge in the third century. Pins with plain heads and some with elaborately carved tops imitating bronze examples were used by peasant women in hair fashions and for fastening clothes. Needles, spindles, armlets, combs and counters were also manufactured.

Clothing

Women would have made most of the clothing for their family. This activity is attested by spindle whorls, spindles, loom shuttles and loom weights. Animal fibres such as wool and vegetable fibres such as flax were used for cloths. Wool production may have expanded in the fourth century under state direction with the chalklands and Brecklands extensively used for grazing. Garments were made in state factories to meet official demands.

Leather working was a more specialised activity. The fens may have supplied the army with a considerable proportion of its requirements. Offcuts have been found near workshops to the south-east of Durobrivae. Shoes were recovered from a well at Lynch Farm and sandals at White Mill Drain, Elm.

Religion

Abandinus is the only native god whose name can be ascribed certainly to one of the several temples known in the region. Three circular structures of the third century in Normangate Field, one with wall-paintings and a tessellated floor, were probably temples. Here also a workshop was converted to a temple with an apse, portico and tessellated floor added. A Romano-Celtic temple was found among the farm buildings at Lynch Farm. A religious function has been ascribed to a second and third century aisled building at King's Hedges which was adorned with sculptured blocks including a representation of a warrior or war god.

Finds of bronze and stone sculptures, most of which must have belonged to shrines, give some indication of the range of native gods and their Roman equivalents that were venerated. The imperial cult seems to have been prominent in the fens. A fine bronze bust of Commodus was found at Bullock's Haste, Cottenham. A statuette of bronze inlaid with silver from Berry Fen, Bluntisham, is in the form of a bearded male figure (probably Jupiter), wearing armour and a Corinthian helmet, and dates to the later second century. Mercury is represented by bronze statuettes from Fenstanton, Manea Fen and Cambridge. Hercules was venerated widely. A stone statue was found at Sibson and bronze statuettes at Ely. Pipeclay figurines of Venus were imported and used as offerings to various female deities: two bronze statuettes of the goddess came from Ely. A stone statue of Minerva was recovered at Sibson.

14. Bronze Imperial bust from the Willingham Fen Hoard *(Courtesy of the Museum of Archaeology and Ethnology, Cambridge University)*

15. Sceptre from the Willingham Fen Hoard *(Courtesy of the Museum of Archaeology and Ethnology, Cambridge University)*

16. Bronze Horsemen, Willingham Fen Hoard *(Courtesy of the Museum of Archaeology and Ethnology, Cambridge University)*

17. Goblet from the Water Newton Hoard *(Copyright British Museum)*

Other deities or mythical creatures represented in bronze statuettes include Diana (Bassingbourn), a Celtic deity (Girton), a genius (Ely) and a satyr (Linton).

A hoard of bronzes deposited in a wooden box at Willingham may have come from a local shrine dedicated to several deities with strong Celtic affinities but also incorporating the imperial cult. The main item was three pieces of one or more maces or sceptres. One section is a knobbed club which may indicate Diana worship at the shrine. The second is a tube with four relief figures; a representation of the Celtic god Taranis identified with the Roman Jupiter, a three-horned bull associated with fertility, a dolphin connected with water cults, appropriate to the fenland landscape and a wheel

18. Inscribed plaque from the Water Newton Hoard *(Copyright British Museum)*

surmounted by an eagle. The third piece is a bust of Antoninus Pius. The other elements in the hoard included fragments of maces, two miniature horsemen (a comparable statuette has been found at Westwood, Peterborough), an owl, eagle, part of a bronze helmetted figure, a bust, facemask, a single-horned boar's head and a bit as well as an amber ring and beads of jet and glass.

The Christian religion is evidenced by the remarkable silver hoard found at Durobrivae. Provisionally dated to the later third century, this is the earliest known find of its kind in the Empire. The vessels were stacked within a wide shallow dish with a chi-rho monogram at its centre. Two bowls had inscriptions at their rims. One read INNOCENTIA ET VIVENTIA

19. Flagon from the Water Newton Silver Hoard *(Copyright British Museum)*

20. Pewter tazza with Christian symbols from Sutton *(Courtesy of the Museum of Archaeology and Ethnology, Cambridge University)*

( )RUNT and the other SANCTVM ALTARE TVVM/DOMINE SUBNIXVS HONORO, the latter having the name PVBLIANVS on its base. The other vessels were a two-handled goblet, a hanging bowl highly decorated with facetting, a flagon elaborately adorned with vine-scroll and palmette motifs, the damaged remains of another flagon and a strainer with a long handle, the terminal of which bore a chi-rho. There were also seventeen triangular votive plaques, seven of which had chi-rhos and one with an inscription ANICILLA VOTVM QVOD PROMISIT COMPLEVIT. The nailing up of such plaques in shrines continues a pagan practice and is a reflection of the fusion of elements of the earlier religion of the Roman populace with the not yet fully-standardised rites of the Christian Church. The only gold object from the hoard was a disc bearing a chi-rho and an alpha and omega symbol. The silverware may have belonged to a church and been buried during a time of persecution.

Another undoubtedly Christian object of fourth-century date is a pewter *tazza* from Ely, possibly a portable font. On the eight-pointed flange are incised a chi-rho, two peahens, a peacock, an owl and sirens. A cursive inscription on the vessel has not been satisfactorily interpreted. Several lead tanks found in the region are thought to have been used in baptismal rites.

45

Burials

Cremation was the common burial rite of the first two centuries although sporadic inhumations are found, as at Guilden Morden, Cherry Hinton and Milton. Some cemeteries, like that of Guilden Morden, were used from Belgic times. Each town had large cemeteries outside its boundary disposed at each side of the roads entering the settlement. Burial grounds were also attached to villa estates. At Litlington a walled enclosure contained rows of cremations. These were deposited in various ways, some in tile cists, others in small flint enclosures, wooden boxes or simple holes in the ground covered by tiles. The standard association of grave goods was the jar containing the cremation accompanied by a flagon or dish. Dishes, often of samian, were used as urn covers. Other goods such as bracelets, brooches, beads and glass vessels were less common. In the corners of the enclosure were piles of ashes from the funeral pyres; tongs for the ashes and an incense shovel illustrate aspects of the burial rite. At Guilden Morden cremation was practised into the fourth century. The objects accompanying the burials were similar to those at Litlington. In one interment the urn was accompanied by other pots, an iron lamp and the hobnails of two shoes. Shoes seem often to have been buried with the deceased. At Girton a wooden casket with bronze fittings in the form of boars' heads contained a hexagonal glass urn with the ashes, and other glass vessels including a bowl of Egyptian origin bearing an incised design of a duck and Nilotic plants, a lead-glazed pot from Gaul, samian and a pottery flagon. A fine Antonine group of glass bottles and samian vessels was found south of Arbury Road, Cambridge.

Several burial plots were graced with sculptured stone funerary monuments. At Girton the figures included a male torso wearing a belted tunic and a lion group. A lion and stag group was found at Durobrivae and two charioteers at Bedford Purlieus.

Inhumation rites superseded cremation during the third century. The same cemeteries were usually used and as the wooden painted markers of many of the earlier graves had become displaced it is not uncommon for the cremations to have been disturbed by later burials. At Guilden Morden the bodies were set facing several directions. Wooden coffins were sometimes used. Often there are no goods but those found included pots and bronze and shale armlets. Some individuals bore the ferryman's coin in their mouths. One person may have been a religious functionary as he was buried with a bronze cylinder with a phallic pendant, an object like a sceptre, an iron ring and ferrule. Several persons had been decapitated, one woman (who may have been regarded as a witch) after death. At Arbury Road there was a small family plot belonging to the nearby villa. In its first phase in the late third century four males were buried, two in wood coffins. In the second an old woman in a shroud was laid in a lead-lined Barnack stone coffin. The burial party seems to have incorrectly orientated the coffin and to correct matters inserted the body and lining into the coffin the wrong way round with the feet at the head end. Later a rectangular, chalk-built mausoleum was erected with a tile roof. This contained an adult male in a lead-lined stone coffin: the coffin as delivered was too small for the intended body and had been broken to accommodate it and the lining.

At Litlington a stone tomb contained a stone coffin burial. In the artisan's zone of Normangate Field the cemetery was disposed at each side of a lane parallel to Ermine Street. Several mausolea were erected. One rectangular one contained three burials, of which one was a female in a stone coffin accompanied by her earrings, brooch, armlets, spindle, bone comb and a jug. Several other coffin burials are known, such as those at Gravel Hill Farm, Cambridge, Stilton and the male burial at Hemingford Abbots accompanied by a third century pot. Three children and two females had been interred in a humbler family plot excavated at Linton. One child had a jet necklace of 148 beads and other goods. Infant burials below the floors of houses are found in the towns and villages.

Burial in a barrow is a feature found particularly in Eastern England, perhaps continuing pre-Roman practices. Few of these are well-documented. That at Lord's Bridge near Hauxton (14.63 metres by 7.32 and 2.59 high), was composed of gravel, gault and yellow sandy clay. A secondary inhumation had been dug into it. In a lidless stone coffin was the primary burial, a female who had been in a dismembered state before she had been interred, her body being accompanied by two bone hairpins, bones of a cock and a goose, a tooth of a sheep and pig and pieces of pot placed around the sides at the wider end of the coffin. Outside the coffin were twenty seven hobnails. This barrow and that at Emmanuel Knoll, Godmanchester, lay by the side of the main road. The latter was 9.75 metres in diameter and 1.83 high. The primary interment was a cremation of early third-century date, the ashes in an urn within a wooden box placed in a shallow pit near the centre of the mound. No burial was detected under the mound at Limlow Hill which was composed of earth and chalk, 12.8 metres in diameter and 5.49 metres high; instead, a flint-filled pit lay at the centre. The barrow was contained within a rectangular enclosure ditch and probably dates to the late second century.

ACKNOWLEDGEMENTS

Photographs in the Museum of Archaeology and Ethnology kindly supplied by Mr G. Owen and Miss J. Liversidge.

Further Reading

Much of our information on Roman Cambridgeshire is scattered in journals or remains unpublished. Excavation reports and descriptions of individual finds can be found in the principal local journals: *Proceedings of the Cambridge Antiquarian Society* and *Transactions of the Cambridgeshire and Huntingdonshire Archaeological Society* now combined with the *CAS Proceedings.*

Summary reports of work in the area can be found conveniently in the annual *Roman Britain in 19..* in the *Journal of Roman Studies* up to 1969 and in *Britannia* from 1970 (Society for the Promotion of Roman Studies).

Early research in the county is well summarised by Cyril Fox, *The Archaeology of the Cambridge Region* (Cambridge, 1923) and in volume I of the *Victoria History of the County of Huntingdon.*

The following books and papers are of prime importance for any study of the county in Roman times. They include all the principal references. I am very pleased to acknowledge my debt to the authors on whose work it will be appreciated I have relied heavily.

For the fens, see C.W. Phillips (ed.), *The Fenland in Roman Times* (London, The Royal Geographical Society, 1970).

For Godmanchester, see H.J.M. Green, *Roman Godmanchester,* in W. Rodwell and T. Rowley (eds.) *Small Towns of Roman Britain,* British Archaeological Reports 15 (Oxford, 1975), 183-210, and the same author's *Godmanchester* (Cambridge, 1978).

For the Nene Valley, see J.P. Wild, *Roman Settlement in the Lower Nene Valley* in *The Archaeological Journal,* 131 (1975), 140-170. The Nene Valley Research Committee has been engaged in work in the valley for many seasons and produces an annual report *Durobrivae,* obtainable from Mrs. C. Mackreth, 32 Hall Lane, Werrington, Cambs.

For Cambridge see D.M. Browne, *An Archaeological Gazetteer of the City of Cambridge* in *Proceedings of the Cambridge Antiquarian Society,* LXV(i) (1974). This paper includes the main references to work in the town, the most important of which is that of Dr John Alexander.

D.M. Browne's forthcoming contribution to the *Victoria County History,* with full references, is the most comprehensive account of the remains from the old county to be produced to date.